Revelation 2-3

A message from Jesus to the church today

by Tim Chester
& Jonathan Lamb

Series Editor: Tim Chester

Revelation 2-3: a message from Jesus to the church today
© Tim Chester/Jonathan Lamb/The Good Book Company, 2007.

The Good Book Company
Tel: 0845-225-0880
Fax: 0845-225-0990
Email: admin@thegoodbook.co.uk
Internet: www.thegoodbook.co.uk

Unless indicated, all Scripture references are taken from the HOLY BIBLE,
NEW INTERNATIONAL VERSION. Copyright © 1973, 1978, 1984 International Bible
Society. Used by permission.

ISBN 13: 9781905564682

Printed in the UK

Contents

Introduction: Good Book Guides

Every Bible-study group is different—yours may take place in a church building, in a home, in a cafe, on a train, over a leisurely mid-morning coffee or squashed into a 30-minute lunch break. Your group may include new Christians, mature Christians, non-Christians, students, business colleagues or teens. That's why we've designed these *Good Book Guides* to be flexible for use in many different situations.

Our aim in each session is to uncover the meaning of a passage, and see how it fits into the 'big picture' of the Bible. But that can never be the end. We also need to apply appropriately what we have discovered to our lives. Let's take a look at what is included:

⊕ **Talkabout:** most groups need to 'break the ice' at the beginning of a session, and here's the question that will do that. It's designed to get people talking around a subject that will be covered in the course of the Bible study.

⬇ **Investigate:** the Bible text for each session is broken up into manageable chunks, with questions that aim to help you understand what the passage is about. **The Leader's Guide** contains **guidance on questions**, and sometimes ⊠ additional 'follow-up' questions.

⊡ **Explore more (optional):** these questions will help you connect what you have learned to other parts of the Bible, so you can begin to understand how the Bible relates together as a whole.

➔ **Apply:** As you go through a Bible study, you'll keep coming across **apply** sections. Some of these have questions to get the group discussing what the Bible teaching means in practice for you and your church. Sometimes, a ⊡ **getting personal** section is an opportunity for you to think, plan and pray about the changes that you personally may need to make as a result of what you have discovered.

⬆ **Pray:** We want to encourage prayer that is rooted in God's Word—in line with His concerns, purposes and promises. So each session ends with an opportunity to review the truths and challenges highlighted by the Bible study, and turn them into prayers of request and thanksgiving.

The **Leader's Guide** and introduction provide historical background information, explanations of the Bible texts for each session, ideas for **optional extra** activities, and guidance on how best to help people uncover the truths of God's Word.

Why study Revelation 2-3?

What message would you give to your local church if you had their undivided attention? Apart from the little niggles that frustrate us and soak up so much emotional energy – would there be a deep underlying issue that you would want to expose?

And what message would you give the wider church? What is the most important thing Christians today need to hear? What would Jesus say to His people today? Thankfully, there is no need to speculate on this question.

In Revelation 2-3 we find out what the risen Christ had to say to seven specific churches. Some of them were facing persecution – just as many Christians today face hostility. The apostle John, who passed on these messages, was himself in exile – a victim of one of the persecutions against Christians that was sweeping the ancient world at the time.

But some of these churches were also compromised. They were being pulled away from following Christ by their culture. They did not face hostility from the outside because, if truth be told, they were not so very different from the world around them.

Jesus brings a message of comfort and hope to those who are suffering for their faith. He brings a wake-up call to those who are compromised. He speaks in love of the love that really matters. Not love for the world, but a deep love for Jesus – and a desire to please Him by the way we live. He tells us what is truly important. He offers great resources to those who remain faithful. He promises great rewards to those who overcome.

To each church He says: 'He who has an ear, let him hear what the Spirit says to the churches.' These seven messages are rooted in the specific challenges faced by each congregation. But they are also a word for every church today. They are not just what the Spirit *spoke* to *a* church. They are what the Spirit *says* to *the churches*. They are what the Spirit is saying in our day to the churches of our day.

Ephesus: Revelation 2 v 1-7

THE CENTRALITY OF LOVE

⊕ talkabout

1. What are the characteristics of a mature, healthy Christian?

⬇ investigate

> **Read Revelation 1 v 9 – 2 v 1**

2. The seven messages in Revelation 2 – 3 are the words of Jesus. How is Jesus described in 1 v 9-20?

3. What is the significance of the description of Jesus in 2 v 1?

❯ Read Revelation 2 v 1-7

4. List the things the risen Christ says the Ephesians have done well.

5. Jesus commends the Ephesians for their hard work (v 2).
What would a hard-working church look like today?

6. Jesus commends the Ephesians for their rejection of false teachers (v 2 and 6). What would this look like in your situation?

7. Jesus commends the Ephesians for their perseverance (v 2-3).
How would a persevering church be different from others?

Verses 2-3 seem to describe model Christians. They are conscientious, doctrinally-sound church members. And yet something is badly wrong in the church at Ephesus. Jesus holds something against them: they have forsaken their first love (v 4).

8. What does it mean to forsake your first love?

9. What does the warning in verse 5 say about conscientious, doctrinally-sound churches that are not passionate about Jesus?

Ephesus was the gateway to Asia Minor. Much of the region's trade passed through its port. A wide road lined with columns on both sides ran from the city down to the harbour. The refinement and wealth of the empire were on full display in Ephesus. It seems that, although the church had not let their thinking be infected by worldly ideas, their hearts *had* been infected by *worldly priorities*. Amazingly, we can be proud of the good teaching in our church and yet have Jesus against us!

⤷ apply

10. What things in church life can compete with Jesus for our first love?

☺ getting personal

If someone kept a record of the way you spend your time and money, what would they conclude about what you love most?

explore more

Read Deuteronomy 8

- What will threaten the faithfulness of the people of Israel?

- What are they told to remember?

- What are they to do that will keep them from ignoring God (v 10)?

- What lessons are there in Deuteronomy 8 for the church in Ephesus

- What lessons are there in this passage for the church in general, an
  yours in particular?

The risen Christ calls on the church to come back to its first love—Jes
Himself. They can rekindle this passion by looking back (v 5) and by
looking forward (v 7).

11. What does it means to 'remember the height from which you have
fallen' (v 5)?

The promise in 2 v 7 looks forward to John's vision of the new creatic
in 22 v 1-5 – the new Jerusalem. The book as a whole presents a
challenge for believers to choose which city they will belong to:
Jerusalem, or Babylon (see 18 v 1-5). Because to choose a city is to
choose a destiny.

12. What does it mean for God's people to 'come out' of Babylon (18 v ⁴

→ **apply**

13. What difference should the vision of 2 v 7 and 22 v 1-5 make to the way we live our lives day by day?

14. What would the risen Christ say to the prosperous church in the west?

15. What changes do you need to make in the light of this message from the risen Christ?

↑ **pray**

- Use the words of Psalm 84 to shape your prayers. Encourage people to take a verse in turn and use it as a basis for a short prayer of praise or request.

Smyrna: Revelation 2 v 8-11

THE PRESSURE OF PERSECUTION

⊕ talkabout

1. When have you faced hostility as a Christian?

An estimated 200 million Christians are facing direct, hostile persecution in the world today. The message to the church of Smyrna was written to believers facing just such persecution.

⬇ investigate

▶ Read Revelation 2 v 8-11

2. How does Jesus describe the circumstances of the church in Smyrna?

3. What does Jesus mean when He tells the Christians in Smyrna that they are rich (v 9)?

4. The Christians in Smyrna are being slandered by some within the Jewi community. Why does Jesus describe these Jews in the way He does?

5. What encouragement is there for the Christians in Smyrna in verse 9?

6. The ten days in verse 10 may be literal or figurative.
What encouragement does this verse give for the Christians in Smyrna?

7. Why does God allow His people to suffer?

8. Verse 10 says some of the Christians will be martyred.
What encouragement is there in this message for Christians who are persecuted 'even to the point of death'?

⤳ apply

9. What commands does Jesus give in this message?

10. When are you tempted to be afraid?
When are you tempted to be unfaithful to Jesus?

11. What encouragement do these verses give us in these circumstances?

⊡ **pray**

• Pray for Christians around the world facing persecution.

• Pray for Christians in your group facing hostility.

• Pray for yourselves that you would remain faithful.

Pergamum: Revelation 2 v 12-17

THE IMPORTANCE OF TRUTH

⊕ talkabout

1. What do you think is the greatest threat facing the church today?

⊕ investigate

❯ Read Revelation 2 v 12-17

2. Jesus tells the church that He knows where they live (v 13). Why is this significant?

Pergamum was full of pagan temples dominated by a massive altar to Zeus on the hill above the city. It was also a centre for worshipping the Roman emperor. The first ever temple in honour of a living emperor, Augustus, was built at Pergamum in 29 BC. This may explain the reference to Pergamum being where Satan lives and has his throne (v 13).

3. What threats has the church faced?

4. What does Jesus mean when He commends the church for 'remaining true to my name'?

The church has remained faithful to Jesus in the face of external threats and hostility. Now the church faces a new threat – a threat from within.

5. What exactly does Jesus rebuke the church for? Why is this important?

6. Balaam was a 'freelance' prophet in the Old Testament. Balak, the king of Moab, hired him to curse the people of Israel. **See Numbers 23 v 1-12.** What happened when Balaam was hired to curse God's people?

7. A direct curse-assault on Israel by the Moabites failed. So the Moabites tried another strategy. **See Numbers 25 v 1-9.** What was that strategy? What was the result?

8. **Read Numbers 31 v 16.** Whose idea was this strategy?

9. **Look at Revelation 2 v 14-15.** The risen Christ compares what is happening in Pergamum to the story of Balaam.
What does this suggest was going on in the church?

10. So what exactly is 'the teaching of Balaam'?

11. What action does Jesus want the church to take?

12. What does the symbolism of Jesus' warning in v 16 imply?

13. How does the promise of manna in verse 17 particularly bring comfort to the church in Pergamum?

> ❯ **Read John 6 v 26-35.** The day before Jesus had miraculously fed 5,000 people. This miracle bread, He explains, is a picture of what He offers: true satisfaction and fulfilment.

• Jesus mentions 'food that spoils' (v 27). What is that a picture of?

• What is the 'food that endures to eternal life'?

⊡ **getting personal**

optional

> ❯ **Read Isaiah 55 v 1-2.**

• What 'food' are you pursuing instead of coming to God's feast?

• What are you 'spending' to pursue it?

• What lasting satisfaction does it bring?

• What will you do to come to God and 'delight in the richest of fare'?

It is not clear to what the white stone in verse 17 refers. Stones were used as tokens of admission – like a ticket – so this may be a picture of the Christian's right to enter God's kingdom. Stones were also used when a jury voted (white for innocent, black for guilty) so this may be a picture of the Christian's acquittal on the day of judgment.

14. How does the promise of a new name in verse 17 bring us comfort?

➔ **apply**

15. What false teaching do you think threatens the church today?

A message from Jesus to the church today

16. The complaint of the risen Christ in v 14 suggests it is not enough to hold to true teaching. We must also stamp out false teaching. What might it mean for you to counter false teaching?

⬆ pray

1 Timothy 3 v 15-16 describes the church as 'the pillar and foundation of the truth'.

- Pray that your church might be a 'pillar and foundation of the truth'.

- Celebrate that truth by praying through each line of Paul's description of the truth in 1 Timothy 3 v 16.

- Close by saying together 2 Timothy 2 v 11-13.

Thyatira: Revelation 2 v 18-29

THE CHALLENGE OF CONSISTENCY

⊕ talkabout

1. What are the biggest challenges you face in your workplace or home?

⊡ investigate

❯ Read Revelation 2 v 18-29

Thyatira was a commercial centre and trading hub (Acts 16 v 14). It was a place with many trade guilds, which were like local chambers of commerce. If you wanted to succeed in business, you needed to be part of a trade guild. But the trade guilds also involved pagan sacrifices and the worship of the emperor.

2. What does the risen Christ praise the church in Thyatira for?

3. Compare 2 v 14-16 with 2 v 20-22. What are the similarities between the warnings given to Pergamum and Thyatira?

4. 'Jezebel' is Christ's name for an influential woman in the church. It is also a particular woman in the Old Testament. Look at **1 Kings 16 v 3 33; 18 v 4, 19; 19 v 1-2** and write a 'CV' of Jezebel.
What was her position? Where was she from? What did she do?

Israel did not worship Baal instead of the Lord. They worshipped Baal *as well as* the Lord. That is why the prophet Elijah says: 'How long will you waver between two opinions?' (1 Kings 18 v 21).

5. What does the comparison with Jezebel reveal about what is going on in the church in Thyatira?

6. What does Jesus' warning to the church imply?

⤷ **apply**

7. Compare the values and priorities of the church with the values and priorities of your workplace or home.
What are the similarities and differences?

8. Compare your *behaviour* in the church with your behaviour in the workplace or home.
What are the similarities and differences?

⊡ **investigate**

9. What is the command of Jesus to the rest of the church?

10. What does Jesus mean by 'Satan's so-called secrets'?

Verse 27 is a quote from **Psalm 2** where Israel's King is called 'God's Son' and given authority over the nations. Jesus says in verse 27 that He is God's King, and God has given him authority. Now Jesus gives that authority to His people.

11. ▶ **Read Matthew 28 v 18-20**
How do believers exercise the authority of Jesus in the world?

Jesus also promises His people 'the morning star'. The morning star is the planet Venus, which appears just before dawn. Venus was also the Roman goddess of victory. According to Revelation 22 v 16, the morning star is a picture of Jesus Himself.

12. What does it mean to say that Jesus is the morning star?

⤏ apply

13. How can we obey the command to 'hold on' until Jesus comes (v 25)?

14. How does the promise of the coming day of victory help us when we face challenges at work or in the home?

⤒ pray

Pray that your life on Mondays might reflect your words on Sunday. Think of what you sung last Sunday and the teaching you heard. Pray specifically that you might live this out in the remainder of the week.

Sardis: Revelation 3 v 1-6

THE EMPTINESS OF REPUTATION

⊕ talkabout

1. What reputation do you think your church has? Do you think it is deserved?

⬇ investigate

❯ Read Revelation 3 v 1-6

2. What reputation does the church in Sardis have in the sight of other people?

3. How does the church look 'in the sight of my God' (v 1-2)?

The city of Sardis was surrounded on three sides by cliffs so the residents felt their city was impregnable. It seems the church suffered from the same complacency. They enjoyed a good reputation, but Jesus offers a very different assessment.

⊡ explore more

Paul talks about living 'in the sight of God' in 2 Corinthians. People he calls 'super-apostles' were threatening God's work among the Corinthia (12 v 11). They appeared flashy and impressive. But Paul says the Corinthians 'are looking only on the surface of things' (10 v 7).

▶ Read 2 Corinthians 2 v 17; 4 v 2; 8 v 19-21; 12 v 19

• What does it means to live 'in the sight of God'?

• What behaviour does it lead to?

▶ Read 2 Corinthians 10 v 12-18 and 11 v 30

• How does Paul say should we assess Christian ministry?

4. The few people in Sardis who are commended by Jesus are commend because they 'have not soiled their clothes' (v 4). What does this sugg about the rest of the church?

⊟ apply

5. What are some of the ways Christians or churches can appear impres without having a genuine or healthy spiritual life?

A message from Jesus to the church today

6. What does the risen Christ tell the church in Sardis to do?

7. This message comes from 'him who holds the seven spirits of God'. Seven = completeness, so 'the seven spirits' = the complete ministry of the Holy Spirit. Why should this description be encouraging to us?

⊡ explore more

'He who has an ear, let him hear what the Spirit says to the churches' (v 6)
• What does this verse tell us about the Bible?

• Whose voice do we hear in the Bible?

• What is the significance of it being addressed to 'the churches' (plural), even though this is a message to one particular church?

• What is the significance of the present tense 'says' instead of the past tense 'said'?

8. What will happen if the church does not repent?

9. What promises does Jesus give to those who do not compromise? What do they mean?

→ apply

10. What practical steps can we take to ensure we remain spiritually alive and spiritually awake (v 1-2)?

11. Should we try to get a good reputation? Why?

↑ pray

O breath of life, come sweeping through us,
revive your church with life and power.
O breath of life, come cleanse renew us,
and fit your church to meet this hour.

Elizabeth Ann Head

THE PAIN OF EXCLUSION

talkabout

1. Can you think of times when you have been 'left out' of something because other people are wary of Christians?

2. What things do believers 'miss out' on because of our different priorities?

⊥ investigate

❯ Read Revelation 3 v 7–13

It seems the Christians in the church at Philadelphia had been excluded from Jewish community life. Jesus says the local synagogue belongs to Satan (v 9).

3. What does Jesus mean when He speaks of those 'who claim to be Jews but are not' (v 9)?

4. How does Jesus describe the Christians in Philadelphia?

5. What does Jesus say that would comfort Christians who feel excluded

6. How would being addressed by the One 'who holds the key of David' comfort the Christians in Philadelphia?

7. How would the picture of an open door comfort the Christians (v 7-8)

8. What does Jesus mean when He says their opponents will fall at the fe of the Christians (v 9)?

A message from Jesus to the church today

9. What does Jesus promise to those in Philadelphia who keep this command?

10. How would the promises of verses 11-12 comfort Christians who feel excluded?

⤷ **apply**

11. How should we respond when we are left out, or when we feel we have missed out because of our faith in Jesus?

12. What would *not* enduring patiently and *not* holding on look like for you?

⤴ **pray**

- Pray for Christians facing pressure to compromise their faith in Jesus.

- Pray for Christians who have been excluded from their families, work or society because of their faith in Jesus.

- Praise God that no one can take our crown and we will never have to leave the presence of God.

Laodicea: Revelation 3 v 14-22

THE DANGER OF SELF-RELIANCE

⊕ talkabout

1. How would you define Christianity?

⊕ investigate

However you define Christianity, one thing is clear: at the centre of Christianity is Jesus. Christianity is all about Jesus.

▶ Read Revelation 3 v 14-22

2. What is the meaning of the symbolic descriptions of Jesus in v 14?

3. How should we respond to such a Jesus?

Hot spring-water was channelled to Laodicea, but by the time the water reached the city it was lime-laden and lukewarm. It was not hot enough to heal, nor cold enough to refresh.

4. What does the comparison with lukewarm water reveal about the church in Laodicea (v 15-16)?

5. Look at verse 17. What was wrong with the church in Laodicea?

☺ **explore more**

▶ **Read Matthew 5 v 3 and 2 Corinthians 12 v 9-10**

• Is it wrong for Christians to feel weak?

• What would you say to a Christian who felt weak?

The city of Laodicea was famous for three things. First, it was a banking centre. With that great wealth came a spirit of independence. The city was devastated by an earthquake in 61AD, but refused help from the Roman emperor. Second, it was a medical centre famous for its eye ointment. Third, it was a clothing centre famous for tunics made from local, glossy black wool.

6. How does the rebuke of Jesus in verse 17 draw on these local features?

7. What does this reveal about the relationship between the church in Laodicea and its surrounding culture?

→ **apply**

8. What is our culture famous for? In what ways is the influence of our culture harming our relationship with Jesus?

⊡ **getting personal**

Think about the way our culture influences you.

• Are there ways in which the world is harming your relationship with Jesus? 'Do not conform any longer to the pattern of this world, but be transformed by the renewing of your mind.' (Romans 12 v 2)

9. Look at verse 20. Where is Jesus? What does this show us about the church in Laodicea?

10. Look at verse 20. What is Jesus doing? What does this show us about Jesus?

11. What does Jesus offer the self-reliant church?

12. Jesus invites us to buy from Him? Look at **Isaiah 55 v 1-2.**
   • What is on the price tag?

13. What might you need to give up to be whole-hearted instead of lukewarm about Jesus?

14. What might you need to do to become more dependent on Jesus and more satisfied in Jesus?

⌷ pray

Look back over our time listening to the message of Jesus to the churches.

1. How have you been encouraged?

2. How have you been challenged?

3. What are you going to do?

Read again the description of the Glory of Jesus in Revelation 1 v 12-16. Then, remembering who you are speaking to, turn your answers into praise and prayer.

Revelation 2-3

a message from Jesus
to the church today

LEADER'S GUIDE

Leader's Guide

Introduction

Leading a Bible study can be a bit like herding cats—everyone has a different idea of what the passage could be about, and a different line of enquiry that they want to pursue. But a good group leader is more than someone who just referees this kind of discussion. You will want to:

★ **correctly understand** and handle the Bible passage. But also…

★ **encourage and train** the people in your group to do this for themselves. Don't fall into the trap of spoon-feeding people by simply passing on the information in the Leader's Guide. Then…

★ make sure that no Bible study is finished without everyone **knowing how the passage is relevant for them**. What changes do you all need to make in the light of the things you have been learning? And finally…

★ encourage the group to turn all that has been learned and discussed into **prayer**.

Your Bible-study group is unique, and you are likely to know better than anyone the capabilities, backgrounds and circumstances of the people you are leading. That's why we've designed these guides with a number of optional features. If they're a quiet bunch, you might want to spend longer on **talkabout**. If your time is limited you can choose to skip **explore more**, or get people to look at these questions at home. Can't get enough of Bible study? Well, some studies have optional extra homework projects. As leader, you can adapt and select the material to the needs of your partic group.

So what's in the Leader's Guide?

The main thing that this Leader's Guide help you to do is to understand the m teaching points in the passage you studying, and how to apply them. As as guidance on the questions, the Lead Guide for each session contains following important sections:

THE BIG IDEA

One key sentence will give you the m point of the session. This is what should be aiming to have fixed in peop minds as they leave the Bible study. And the point you need to head back towa when the discussion goes off at a tang

SUMMARY

An overview of the passage, includ plenty of useful historical backgro information.

OPTIONAL EXTRA

Usually this is an introductory activity, ties in with the main theme of the B study, and is designed to 'break the ice the beginning of a session. Or it may b 'homework project' that people can tac during the week.

So let's take a look at the various feat of a Good Book Guide.

⊕ **talkabout**: each session kicks with a discussion question, based on group's opinions or experiences. designed to get people talking thinking in a general way about the m subject of the Bible study.

⊡ **investigate**: the first thing that you and your group need to know is what the Bible passage is about, which is the purpose of these questions. But watch out —people may come up with answers based on their experiences or teaching they have heard in the past, without referring to the passage at all. It's amazing how often we can get through a Bible study without actually looking at the Bible!

And if you're stuck for an answer the Leader's Guide contains guidance on questions. These are the answers to which you need to direct your group. This information isn't meant to be read out to people—ideally, you want them to discover these answers from the Bible for themselves. Sometimes optional follow-up questions (see ☑ in guidance on questions) are included, to help you help your group get to the answer.

⊡ **explore more**: these questions generally point people to other relevant parts of the Bible. They are useful for helping your group to see how the passage fits into the 'big picture' of the whole Bible. These sections are **OPTIONAL**—only use them if you have time. Remember, it's better to finish in good time having really grasped one big thing from the passage, than to try and cram everything in.

⊡ **apply**: we want to encourage you to spend more time working at application— too often, it is simply tacked on at the end. In the **Good Book Guides**, apply sections are mixed in with the investigate sections of the study. We hope that people will realise that application is not just an optional extra, but rather, the whole purpose of studying the Bible. We do Bible study so that our lives can be changed by what we hear from God's Word. If you skip the application, the Bible study hasn't achieved its purpose.

These questions draw out practical lessons that we can all learn from the Bible passage. You can review what has been learned so far, and think about practical differences that this should make in our churches and our lives. The group gets the opportunity to talk about what they personally have learned.

A ☺ **getting personal** section can be done at home, or you could allocate a few moments of quiet reflection for each person to think about specific changes that they need to make and pray through in their own lives.

Why not have a time for reporting back at the beginning of the following session, so that everyone can be encouraged and challenged by one another to make application a priority?

⊡ **pray**: In Acts 4 v 25-30 the first Christians quoted Psalm 2 as they prayed in response to the persecution of the apostles by the Jewish religious leaders. Today however, it's not as common for Christians to base prayers on the truths of God's Word as it once was. As a result, our prayers tend to be weak, superficial and self-centred rather than bold, visionary and God-centred.

The prayer section is based on what has been learned from the Bible passage. How different our prayer times would be if we were genuinely responding to what God has said to us through His Word.

1

Ephesus: Revelation 2 v 1-7
THE CENTRALITY OF LOVE

THE BIG IDEA
We can be conscientious and doctrinally-sound, but still displease Jesus if we lack heart-felt love.

SUMMARY
The seven messages in Revelation 2-3 have features common to most of them:
- a reminder of who speaks to the church
- a commendation
- a complaint
- a command
- a call to listen to the Spirit, and
- a promise to those who overcome.

People often call them 'letters', but Revelation describes them as 'words' or 'messages'. They are not separate letters, but part of the book of Revelation as a whole. They each begin with a reminder of John's vision of the risen Christ in 1 v 9-20. And they each end with a promise that points forward to some aspect of John's vision in the rest of the book. Some of John's readers were facing persecution (1 v 9; 2 v 9, 13). But persecution was not widespread or systematic when Revelation is most likely to have been written (in the 90s AD).

In part, John is preparing Christians for what might come. But John is also concerned about Christians who are compromising with the culture. The seven churches to whom he writes are all in Asia Minor (modern-day Turkey). It was in Asia Minor (rather than in Rome) that the practice of worshipping Caesar as a god began. People pledged allegiance to

Caesar as Lord, called him 'the son o[f] god', and praised him for bringing pe[ace] and prosperity to the world – all in con[flict] with the claims of Jesus Christ. It se[ems] some Christians participated in [the] 'imperial cult' to get on in life. Others w[ere] seduced by the wealth that Rome ha[d to] offer. The book of Revelation is a criti[que] of imperial idolatry and injustice. It g[ives] us an alternative vision of the n[ew] Jerusalem. This is where our allegia[nce] belongs.

Ephesus was the gateway to Asia Mi[nor]. Much of the region's trade passed thro[ugh] its port. A wide road lined with colu[mns] on both sides ran from the city dow[n to] the harbour. The refinements [and] enticements of the empire were on [full] display in Ephesus – just like the pos[ters] that line our streets and the adverts t[hat] fill our television screens.

In 2 v 2-3 the Ephesians are pra[ised] because they have:
- worked hard (2 v 2)
- rejected false teaching (2 v 2, 6)
- kept going (2 v 3)
They are the conscientious, doctrina[lly] sound church members of their day!

But the church at Ephesus is also war[ned] (2 v 4-5). They have withstood the ass[ault] of false teachings, but they have [not] withstood the seduction of the wo[rld]. Fitting in, and getting on, in the Ro[man] Empire involved joining in with [the] imperial cult and other pagan practi[ces]. We do not know for sure what

Nicolaitans in verse 6 taught, but it is likely they said participation in the imperial cult was okay for Christians (2 v 14-15) – perhaps by arguing that idols were nothing. The Ephesian Christians had not quite gone that far, but they were being seduced. We can pride ourselves on not letting our theology be infected by worldly ideas. But all the time our lives can be infected by worldly priorities. We can live for the things of this world and seek our security in them.

The risen Christ calls on the church to come back to its first love = Jesus Himself.

How can they rekindle this passion?

1. By looking back. 'Remember the height from which you have fallen!' (2 v 5) They are to remember the enthusiasm they had when they first became Christians. They are to remember God's goodness to them on the cross and in their own personal experience.

2. By looking forward (2 v 7). Verse 7 looks forward to John's vision of the new Jerusalem (22 v 1-5). John calls the Roman empire 'Babylon the Prostitute' (18 v 1-3). (Babylon was the Old Testament epitome of human society in opposition to God.) Christians are to 'come out of her' (18 v 4-5). What is the alternative? Where can they go? The alternative is the new Jerusalem. We live for the new creation (21 v 1-5). 'Do not store up for yourselves treasures on earth … But store up for yourselves treasures in heaven.' (Matthew 6 v 19-20)

GUIDANCE ON QUESTIONS

1. There is no need to 'correct' any of the suggestions made in response to this question. Let the study itself fill out people's initial responses.

2. Encourage people to identify all the different descriptions of Jesus in chapter 1: dressed in a robe, with a golden sash, the First and the Last, and so on.

• **What impression does this description give overall?**

• **How would you summarise what it tells us about Jesus?**

3. The seven stars are the angels of the churches (perhaps their leaders or perhaps angels appointed to protect each church) and the seven lampstands are the seven churches themselves (1 v 20). Jesus holds them and walks among them, that is, He is the glorious One described in chapter 1 protects the churches and is with the churches.

4. The risen Christ commends the Ephesians for three things:
• their hard work, v 2;
• their rejection of false teachers, v 2;
• their perseverance, v 3.

5. This is an opportunity to describe *in practice* what Jesus commends. Answers might include people who are quick to volunteer or who serve faithfully over many years in a role. Encourage people to think not only of serving in the church, but also of serving Jesus in the workplace, family and community. This might be an opportunity to honour specific individuals, especially if their roles are not 'up front'.

6. Our culture is uncomfortable with the rejection of views. Biblical tolerance is loving people with views we consider to be wrong. But tolerance today has become pretending that *all* views are valid. So we are in a situation where condemnation is counter-cultural. The fact that Jesus commends the Ephesians for their rejection of false teachers suggests that we must not only teach what is true, but also expose what is false.

7. Think of examples of serving Jesus both in the face of opposition and in the face of disappointment.

8. 'First love' could refer to first in time; ie: you have lost the enthusiasm for Jesus you had when you first became a Christian. Or 'first love' could refer to first in priority; ie: there is now something in your life that you love more than Jesus. It may be a combination of both ideas: the Ephesians used to love Jesus best, but now they love other things more.

9. Jesus warns He will close down the church if it does not repent of its lovelessness. This suggests it is possible to be a conscientious, doctrinally-sound church that is not really a true church at all!

10. There are a number of answers to this question: family, friends, possessions, career. Most are not wrong in themselves, but they must not come before Jesus in our affections. The goods on display by the roadside in Ephesus are like the posters that line our streets and the adverts that fill our television screens.

EXPLORE MORE: The prosperity the people enjoy in the land will threaten their faithfulness. They will no longer feel they need God (v 14, 17). So they are to remember all that God has done for them (v 2-5, 11, 18). They are to praise God for their prosperity because this confirms the land is a gift from Him (v 10).

11. The Christians in Ephesus are remember the enthusiasm they had wh they first became Christians. They are remember God's goodness to them on cross and the new identity that God g them. They are to remember they children of God rather than children of empire.

12. John is clearly referring to the Ron empire when he describes Babylon Prostitute (Babylon was the Old Testam epitome of human society in opposition God). John's readers cannot literally le the Roman empire anymore than should live in a ghetto. Instead, we are come out of the 'value system' of world around us. We are to have differ priorities and different lifestyles. Baby first love is for wealth, power, fame personal glory. *We are to have a differ first love.*

13. 'Do not store up for yoursel treasures on earth … But store up yourselves treasures in heaven.' (Matth 6 v 19-20) See also 1 Corinthians 15 v 32, 58.

14. This is a chance to summarise what have seen from Revelation 2 v 1-7.

● **What do you think the risen Chris saying to our church or group?**

15. Encourage people to suggest spec changes – both for themselves person and for your group as a whole.

OPTIONAL EXTRAS

1. Compare John's vision of Babylon the Prostitute with his vision of Jerusalem the Bride. Read out the description of Babylon the Prostitute in the left-hand column and invite people to identify how Jerusalem the Bride is different, using the verse references in the right-hand column.

BABYLON THE PROSTITUTE	JERUSALEM THE BRIDE
the fornicating prostitute (17 v 2)	the pure bride (21 v 9)
splendour from exploitation (17 v 4; 18 v 12-13, 16)	splendour from God's glory (21 v 22-23)
corrupting and deceiving the nations (17 v 2; 18 v 3; 19 v 2)	a light to the nations (21 v 24)
luxurious wealth extorted from the nations (18 v 12-17)	the nations give their glory (21 v 26)
full of abominations, impurities, deceptions (17 v 4, 5; 18 v 2-3)	uncleanness, abomination and falsehood are excluded (21 v 27)
wine that makes the nations drunk (14 v 8; 17 v 2; 18 v 3)	water of life and the tree of life for the healing of the nations (21 v 6; 22 v 1-2)
God's people are called to come out of her (18 v 4)	God's people are called to enter her (22 v 14)

2. Trace the common features in each message: the reminder of the speaker, the commendation, the complaint, the command and the promise to those who overcome. (Be warned: not every feature is present in every message.) See if you can link the description of the speaker back John's vision in 1 v 9-20 and see if you link the promise to what comes Revelation. Use the table below to b up a picture of what happens over weeks to come.

CHURCH	SPEAKER	COMMENDATION	COMPLAINT	COMMAND	PROMIS
Ephesus 2 v 1-7 (see 22 v 2)					
Smyrna 2 v 8-11 (see 20 v 6)					
Pergamum 2 v 12-17 (see 14 v 1; 22 v 4)					
Thyatira 2 v 18-29 (see 19 v 15; 22 v 16)					
Sardis 3 v 1-6 (see 20 v 12)					
Philadelphia 3 v 7-13 (see 14 v 1; 21 v 2, 22)					
Laodicea 3 v 14-22 (see 20 v 4; 22 v 3)					

2 Smyrna: Revelation 2 v 8-11
THE PRESSURE OF PERSECUTION

THE BIG IDEA
The presence of Christ, the control of God and the promise of eternal life enable us to be faithful under pressure.

SUMMARY
Smyrna is now called Izmir, the second city of Turkey. It had an excellent harbour, flourishing trade and is a beautiful city built around a hill with fine public buildings along the summit – referred to by one second-century writer as 'the crown of Smyrna'. In 26AD Smyrna successfully competed against 11 other cities to be the host city for a new temple built to deify the Emperor Tiberias and it became a centre of the imperial cult.

The small church in Smyrna was facing persecution. Unlike most of the other messages, there is no word of complaint – just pastoral encouragement for struggling Christians. They face the pressures of poverty (2 v 9), slander (2 v 9) and direct persecution (2 v 10). These are the costs of discipleship. But the risen Christ reminds them of the certainties of discipleship.

- **The certainty of Christ's presence.** Christ says: 'I know your afflictions' (2 v 9). In John's vision of the glorified Christ, Christ is 'among' the lampstands, ie: the churches (1 v 13, 20).
- **The certainty of God's control.** The Christians are persecuted by Satan (2 v 9-10). There is a battle between God and Satan (see chapter 12). But God is in

control. He has determined that the persecution will be for a limited period (2 v 10). (Numbers in the book of Revelation are usually symbolic so 'ten days' probably represents a defined period rather than ten literal 24-hour periods.)
- **The certainty of eternal reward** (2 v 8, 10-11). Jesus 'died and came to life again'. Our future hope is based on this past event. It means we need not fear death. The crown may refer to the victory crown of Romans games or the laurel crown given for civic service. It may echo the 'crown of the city' high on the hill. But probably it refers to the royal crown, the reward to faithful disciples who will rule with Christ. The second death is eternal punishment (20 v 14).

These certainties make possible the commands of this message: 'Do not be afraid … Be faithful' (2 v 10).

GUIDANCE ON QUESTIONS
1. Some of us have never faced serious hostility because we are Christians. Other studies in this series will question whether this might be because we are too timid or compromised. For now it is enough to say that *all* Christians need to be ready to face hostility, because it is part of the 'deal' of belonging to Christ.

2. The Christians in Smyrna are poor (v 9) – the word means 'destitute'. Their poverty may be directly related to their profession of Christ (see Hebrews 10 v 33). They are slandered. And they are about to face imprisonment and maybe even death (v 10).

3. We are not told explicitly what it means for the Christians to be rich. We know it cannot mean economic wealth since they are economically poor. It must refer to the riches they have in Christ – a relationship with God and the hope of heaven (see James 2 v 5). Today the church is often growing rapidly in those parts of the world where it is economically poor.

4. Many of the converts to Christianity probably come from a Jewish background. As a result, the leaders of the Jewish community seem to be threatened or jealous so they are slandering the Christians to the Roman authorities. Jesus says they are not true Jews, ie: they do not deserve to be seen as the people of God. They are 'a synagogue of Satan', ie: doing Satan's work. Satan is called 'the accuser' (Revelation 12 v 10).

EXPLORE MORE: The dragon in Revelation 12 represents Satan (12 v 9). He attacks Christ (12 v 4); he leads the world astray (12 v 9); he accuses Christians (12 v 10) as he did in Smyrna (2 v 9); and he wars against the church (12 v 17). We need not fear Satan because he has been defeated (12 v 8-9), but we must take him seriously because he continues to rage against the church (12 v 12, 17; see also 1 Peter 5 v 8-9). We overcome him by the blood of the Lamb: Satan's accuses us of belonging to hell because of our sin, but the blood of Jesus makes us righteous (12 v 11). And we overcome Satan by the word of our testimony: by our proclamation of the gospel even in the face of death (12 v 11).

EXPLORE MORE: This is an opportunity remind one another of the reality of Sa and his work against the church. We ne not fear Satan because he has be defeated, but we should take h seriously because he still seeks to dev Christians. We should not retaliate wh people slander us. Instead we should good, trust God and rejoice that we sh in Christ's sufferings.

5. Twice in verse 9 Jesus says, 'I know .

- **Where is Jesus in John's vision chapter 1?** See 1 v 13 where lampstands = the churches.

- **How does Jesus knowing o situation encourage us when we f problems?** See 2 Timothy 4 v 17-18 a Hebrews 4 v 15.

6. Jesus knows about their suffering advance and He knows that it will e The ten days may refer to the length athletic games or gladiatorial contests which Christians would be victims, or t may refer to a short period of time (like saying 'a couple of weeks'). However understand them, they suggest that suffering of the Christians has a defir limit. It will come to an end. Satan only attack God's people with Go permission (Job 1 v 12). God is in contr even when we are suffering and e when Satan is at work.

7. See Philippians 1 v 12-14 and James 2-4. We do not fully know why God all suffering. But we do know that God u our suffering for His glory, the spread of gospel and the maturing of His people.
8.

• **See verse 8.** How is Jesus described? (See 1 v 17-18.) Graffiti found by archaeologists in Rome reads: 'Rome, your power will never end.' It must have felt like Roman power was the last word in history. But Jesus is the First and the Last. And Jesus has 'died and come to life again'. Our future hope is based on this past event. It means we need not fear death.

• **See verse 10.** Jesus will give 'the crown of life'. This may refer to the victory crown of Roman games or the laurel crown given for civic service. Or it may refer to Smyrna itself. Smyrna (modern-day Izmir) was a beautiful city overtopped by a hill with fine public buildings along the summit – referred to as 'the crown of Smyrna'. Allegiance to Rome offered many rewards, but Jesus offers a crown of life – eternal life. The 'crown of life' probably refers to the royal crown, the reward to faithful disciples who will rule with Christ.

• **See verse 11.** The Christians in Smyrna may have to face (the first) death, but they will escape the second death.

• **What is the second death? See 20 v 14.** The second death is eternal punishment. Notice the words 'not … at all'. This is emphatic: whatever happens to us in this life, ultimately we will be eternally secure.

9. See verse 10: 'Do not be afraid … Be faithful'.

11. This is an opportunity to summarise what we have learnt from this message.

• **These verses were spoken to Christians facing martyrdom (see also 12 v 11). What message do they have for those of us who are unlikely to face martyrdom?** Death is the ultimate enemy. If we need not fear death then we need not fear lesser threats. The hope of eternal reward should outweigh all earthly rewards we might lose because we are Christians.

OPTIONAL EXTRAS

1. Ask someone to research persecuted Christians to introduce the passage or for prayer.

2. Ask someone to research the story of Polycarp, a disciple of John and a member of the church in Smyrna, who was martyred in 156 AD. His words on facing death are inspiring.

3 Pergamum: Revelation 2 v 12-17
THE IMPORTANCE OF TRUTH

THE BIG IDEA

We not only need to hold true teaching; we also need to counter false teaching.

SUMMARY

Jesus begins by telling the church at Pergamum that He knows where they live, ie: He knows the context in which they live with its pressures (v 13) and temptations (v 14-16). Pergamum was a religious centre, full of pagan temples dominated by a massive altar to Zeus on the hill above the city. It was also a centre for the imperial cult. The first ever temple in honour of a living emperor, Emperor Augustus, was built at Pergamum in 29 BC. This may explain the reference to Pergamum being where Satan lives and has his throne (v 13). Jesus commends the church for remaining true to His name in the face of persecution. One of them, Antipas, had been martyred. But still the Christians had refused to renounce their faith.

But it seems the church no longer faced direct persecution ('in the days of …' looks back to a past event). Now they faced a new threat: a threat from within; the threat of false teaching.

The story of Balaam is found in Numbers 22-25. Balak, the king of Moab, asks Balaam to prophesy against God's people. But Balaam finds he can only speak a blessing from God (see Numbers 23 v 11-12). Direct attack fails. But Balaam suggests another approach (Numbers 31 v 16). Moabite women seduce the men of Israel, leading them into immorality a then into idol worship. Corruption fro within succeeds. Satan's direct attack the church in Pergamum has failed. B now there is a danger of being corrupt from within. Probably the Nicolaitans those who hold Balaam's teaching) a suggesting Christians could join in w the imperial cult and other pagan ritual.

As things stand only a few people ho this teaching, but the majority have r taken steps to stamp it out (v 14). If th do not act, then the risen Christ Hims says He will 'fight against them with th sword of my mouth' (v 12, 16).

These verses reveal Satan's two strategie
• To turn the world against the church (v 13)
• To turn the church against the truth (v 14-16)

Jesus gives three promises to those wh overcome by remaining true to His nam and to His Word (v 17):
• **Hidden manna.** Manna was the foc God gave His people in the wildernes Better than food offered to idols symbol of participation in idolatry) God's feast of manna (a symbol participation in Jesus). See Isaiah 55 v 2 and John 6 v 31-35.
• **A white stone.** It is not clear to wh the white stone refers. Stones were use as tokens of admission so this may be picture of the Christian's right to ente God's kingdom. Stones were used whe

a jury voted (white for innocent, black for guilty) so this may be a picture of the Christian's acquittal on the day of judgment.

• **A new name.** See 14 v 1 and 22 v 4. The new name is a picture of being owned (maybe even 'branded') by God with all the security that entails.

GUIDANCE ON QUESTIONS

1. There is probably no one correct answer to this question. You may want to highlight the way these threats divide into external threats (the hostility of the world) and internal threats (false teaching and corrupt practice).

2. Pergamum was where 'Satan has his throne'. It was a place of threat for the Christians. Jesus knows the context in which they live.

3. The church has faced opposition inspired by Satan. In the past this has included martyrdom for a Christian called Antipas (v 13).

4. The church has remained true to the name of Jesus and has not renounced its faith (v 13).

5. The church has people who hold false teaching. (The next questions explore what this false teaching involves.) Explore with people exactly what Jesus rebukes the church for. The problem is not that the church as a whole holds false teaching. The problem is that the church allows some people to hold false teaching without, it seems, acting to stop them.

6. Balaam could only speak words from God and God gave him a blessing to pronounce on Israel. This happened repeatedly (23 v 5

– 24 v 25). You may also want to read Numbers 22 to get the full story. If you are short of time, summarise this story and the next for the group.

7. Moabite women seduced the men of Israel, leading them into sexual immorality and then into idol worship. As a result, God sent a plague on the people.

9. A direct assault against the people of Israel failed, but corruption from within succeeded. Satan's direct attack on the church in Pergamum had failed. But now there was a danger of being corrupted from within. For John's readers, eating food sacrificed to idols meant participating in the imperial cult and other pagan ceremonies. Sexual immorality could refer to pagan rituals, but immorality is used elsewhere in Revelation as a picture of spiritual adultery (17 v 1-2). Probably the Nicolaitans (= those who hold Balaam's teaching) were suggesting Christians could join in with the imperial cult and other pagan rituals. Participating in this way would enable Christians to avoid persecution and get on in life.

10. The teaching of Balaam suggests it is okay for Christians to hold worldly values and participate in worldly practices.

11. See verse 16. Likening the teaching of the Nicolaitans to the teaching of Balaam reveals how serious the situation is. Jesus calls on the church to repent. For them, this means stamping out the false teaching.

12. Jesus says He will come against the church with 'the sword of his mouth' (v 16). See verse 12 (and 1 v 16). The sword symbolises the authority of God's king to rule and judge (see Isaiah 11 v 4; 49 v 2; Revelation 19 v 15). (Balaam is also threatened with the 'drawn sword' of 'the angel of the LORD' if he curses God's people; Numbers 22 v 23, 31.)

13. Manna was the food God miraculously sent for the Israelites in the wilderness (Exodus 16). The church is tempted to eat food offered to idols, ie: to participate in pagan worship so they are included in the community and enjoy the blessings of the world. Jesus offers a different food to eat – to participate in true worship, be in God's community and enjoy the blessings of the world to come.

EXPLORE MORE: The food that spoils is sin. Sin promises to satisfy us, but it always spoils. The food Jesus offers is Himself. He is the bread of life (v 35). He truly satisfies – now and eternally.

14. See 14 v 1 and 22 v 4. The new na_ is a picture of being owned (maybe e_ 'branded') by God with all the security t_ entails.

15.

⌄

• **What false teaching do you th_ threatens *your* church or group?**

16. It might be helpful to distingu_ between immature Christians who ne_ gentle instruction and false teachers w_ need to be opposed.

OPTIONAL EXTRA
Beforehand invite someone to prepare_ retell the story of Balaam in Numbers _ 25. Encourage them to add their o_ colour and life to the story while retain_ all the key facts. Ask them to retell _ story before turning to question 6.

Thyatira: Revelation 2 v 18-29
THE CHALLENGE OF CONSISTENCY

BIG IDEA
Our lives on Monday mornings should be consistent with what we profess on Sunday mornings.

SUMMARY
Thyatira was a commercial centre and trading hub. Lydia, the first convert in Philippi, was 'a dealer in purple cloth from the city of Thyatira' (Acts 16 v 14). It was a place with many trade guilds, which were like local chambers of commerce. If you wanted to succeed in business, you needed to be part of a trade guild. But the trade

guilds also involved pagan rituals a_ sacrifices. Verse 20 talks about 'eating fc_ sacrificed to idols.' Not only that, but _ trade guilds were steeped in the imperial c_ (see the comments on Ephesus).

The church in Thyatira had much _ commend it (2 v 19). But it was also allow_ compromise in its midst. 'Jezebel' is proba_ Christ's name for an influential woman in _ church. Queen Jezebel was the fore_ queen who introduced the worship of B_ to God's people in the Old Testament, a_ persecuted God's prophets (1 Kings 16 v _

33; 18 v 4, 19; 19 v 1-2). Israel did not worship Baal *instead of* the LORD. They worshipped Baal *as well as* the LORD. That is why the prophet Elijah calls on them to stop wavering between two opinions (1 Kings 18 v 21). Christ uses the name Jezebel to show that the same divided loyalty is going on in Thyatira. People worship Jesus on Sundays, but participate in the imperial cult on Mondays. The 'immorality' in verses 20-21 may refer to pagan rituals, but Revelation uses immorality as a picture of spiritual adultery (17 v 1-2; 18 v 2-3; 19 v 1-3).

People can appear to be respected members of their local church while their work lives or their inner lives are stories of compromise. But the risen Christ has eyes of blazing fire (2 v 18), which search our hearts and minds (2 v 23). In the Old Testament Jezebel's children were all slaughtered. Whether verses 22-23 are literal or not, in this life or the life to come, the meaning is clear: compromise leads to judgment.

Jesus tells the church to:

1. **'Hold on' to the gospel (2 v 25).** Jezebel offers 'Satan's so-called deep things (NIV: 'secrets) '. It may be ironic. Jezebel may have talked about knowing deep secrets *of God*, but Christ says they are really from Satan. Or it may be Jezebel claimed to know the ways of Satan so that she and her followers could take part in pagan rituals without being affected. The point is clear: people offering 'advanced' teaching can sound impressive, but Christians are to remain faithful to the gospel.

2. **Hold on to the heavenly perspective (2 v 26-29).** Jesus gives us authority to proclaim His name (Matthew 28 v 18-20). We will overcome the nations through our suffering witness (see 12 v 5, 10-11).

Jesus also gives us the morning star, ie: Himself (22 v 16). The morning star was the planet Venus, the Roman goddess of victory. Jesus is the sign that God's ultimate day of victory is dawning.

GUIDANCE ON QUESTIONS

2. See verse 19. Christ commends his people for their love and faith, their service and perseverance. They are also 'now doing more than you did at first'. Here was a church that was making progress and growing.

3. Both churches tolerate false teachers (even if the whole church does not follow them). Both false teachings justify participation in pagan worship. Both are warned to repent, otherwise Christ will come to judge. Both are compared to an Old Testament story to highlight how serious the situation is.

4. Queen Jezebel was the foreign queen who introduced the worship of Baal to God's people in the Old Testament, and persecuted God's prophets.

5. Jezebel is *within* the church. She calls herself a Christian. But she claims that it is okay for Christians to join in pagan sacrifices and rituals. The same divided loyalty that Elijah confronted is going on in Thyatira. People worship Jesus on Sundays, but participate in the imperial cult on Mondays. The 'immorality' in verses 20-21 may refer to pagan rituals, but Revelation uses immorality as a picture of spiritual adultery (17 v 1-2; 18 v 2-3; 19 v 1-3).

6. See verses 22-23. Jesus will come in judgment against those who follow Jezebel ('her children') unless they repent. In the OT Jezebel's children were all slaughtered.

Whether verses 22-23 are literal or not, in this life or the life to come, the meaning is clear: compromise leads to judgment.

7. This question is a general question about the culture of our workplaces and homes; the next question makes this personal to our own behaviour and attitudes.

☑
• **What matters most in your workplace or home?**
• **What are the goals?**
• **How do people treat others?**
• **How do people respond to problems?**
• **How do people respond to differences?**
• **What value is given to truth-telling and integrity?**

9. Jesus tells the church to 'hold on' to the gospel (2 v 25).

10. 'Satan's so-called deep things' may be ironic: Jezebel may have talked about knowing deep secrets *of God*, but Christ says they are really from Satan. Or it may be she claimed to know the ways of Satan so that they could take part in pagan rituals without being affected. The point is clear: people offering 'advanced' teaching can sound impressive, but Christians must remain faithful to the gospel.

11. Because all authority has been given to Jesus, he sends us out to the nations to call on them to submit to his authority. We exercise the authority if Jesus by proclaiming the message of Jesus. We call on people to obey his teaching.

☑
John also quotes Psalm 2 v 9 in Revelation 12 v 5. How do Christians overcome in Revelation 12 v 10-11? We overcome through our suffering witness.

12. Jesus is the sign that God's ultimate day of victory is dawning.

13. We 'hold on' by continuing to trust Jesus and His promise of future glory. It involves maintaining and proclaiming the gospel. It means rejecting 'advanced' knowledge or 'deep secrets'. To do this we need to study the source of truth, ie: the Bible. We also need to encourage one another in the truth (Hebrews 3 v 12-13).

14. See, for example, 2 Corinthians 4 v 16-18; 1 Peter 1 v 3-9 and Revelation 14 v 13.

OPTIONAL EXTRAS

1. It has been said that Christians do not tell lies; they sing them. Invite people to flick through your song book, identifying affirmations we make in song that might be at odds with the reality of our lives. For example, how often are the following lines by Isaac Watts an accurate description of our lives?

When I survey the wondrous cross
on which the Prince of glory died,
my richest gain I count but loss,
and pour contempt on all my pride.

The point is not that people should not sing such words. They express that to which we aspire. The point is that we need to sing these words as our serious heartfelt and genuine aspirations – even if at times we fall short of the reality!

2. Beforehand invite someone to prepare to retell the story of Elijah at Mount Carmel in 1 Kings 18 v 16-46. Encourage them to add their own colour and life to the story while retaining all the key facts. Invite them to retell the story after question 4.

Sardis: Revelation 3 v 1-6
THE EMPTINESS OF REPUTATION

BIG IDEA
We must not put our confidence in reputations, but in the life-giving work of God's Spirit.

SUMMARY
The city of Sardis was built above the Hermus valley, an acropolis that was like a giant watchtower, surrounded on three sides by cliffs. So the residents felt their city was impregnable. It seems the church suffered from the same complacency. They felt themselves to be secure, so Jesus has to wake them up (v 2). Unlike the previous churches, Jesus has nothing to commend the church at Sardis about. Not that the church is without people who commend it: it has a reputation as a 'living' or 'lively' congregation. It was the kind of church that has a large congregation, a full programme, a healthy budget and an impressive website. But in reality it was dead (v 1). Christ says: 'I have not found your deeds complete in the sight of God' (v 2). The same idea appears in 2 Corinthians where Paul talks of carrying out his work under God's watching eye with God as his witness. What matters is not the impressive rhetoric or glossy image of the so-called super-apostles in Corinth, but authentic service in God's sight.

Verse 4 reveals what was going on. Christ says that there are a few believers 'who have not soiled their clothes'. Sardis had a reputation for bad character and it seemed that, despite their good image, the church had compromised with the culture of the

city. This compromise might take the form of nominalism, activism, formalism or pharisaism. Each can look impressive, but they are all empty of real spiritual life.

It is not too late. The risen Christ calls on the church to
- **'Wake up and strengthen'** (v 2), ie: nurture spiritual life through the Word of God.
- **'Remember and repent'** (v 3), ie: the church must remember what it has heard (the life-giving Word) and what it has received (the life-giving Spirit).

This message comes from the one who holds the seven spirits of God (seven = completeness, so 'the seven spirits' = the complete ministry of the Holy Spirit in regeneration and renewal.)

If the church does not repent, then Jesus will come like a thief in the night. This may be an allusion to the army of Cyrus, who centuries before had taken the city of Sardis unexpectedly by creeping up the cliffs. In the Gospels this is a reference to Jesus' second coming, but here it may mean His coming in history to remove the lampstand of Sardis, as He also warned He might do in Ephesus (2 v 5).

The risen Christ gives three promises to those who overcome:
- 'dressed in white' – an image of purity
- 'walk with me' – an image of friendship
- 'his name in the book of life' – an image of security

GUIDANCE ON QUESTIONS

2. The church has a good reputation – a reputation for being alive.

• **How might we express this in contemporary language?** It has the reputation of being a 'living' or 'lively' church.

3. Jesus says that, despite its reputation for being alive, the church is dead (v 1). Their deeds are incomplete (v 2), ie: they do not fulfil God's expectations.

• **Jesus normally commends each church. How does He commend the church in Sardis?** Jesus does not commend the church as whole, although He does commend a few people within it (v 4).

EXPLORE MORE: Living in the sight of God means being aware that God sees both our actions and motives. So we do not 'do' ministry for financial gain (2 v 17) or use deceit (4 v 2). Although we will want to set a good example (8 v 21), the commendation of God is what matters most to us (see 1 Corinthians 4 v 1-5). So we speak and act knowing that God sees what we do (12 v 19). We do not assess our ministry by comparing it to other people (10 v 12), but in terms of gospel faithfulness (10 v 14) and gospel fruit (10 v 15-16, 18). Ultimately, our boast is in Christ (10 v 17; see also 1 Corinthians 1 v 28-31).

4. Sardis had a reputation for bad character but, despite its good image, the church had compromised with the culture of the city. Soiled clothes could be an image of corruption. It might refer to the righteousness with which Christ clothes us (Romans 13 v 14; Revelation 16 v 15), which many Christians in Sardis had now compromised.

5. A false reputation can arise from:
• **nominalism** – people attend churc[h] regard themselves as Christians witho[ut] real relationship with Jesus;
• **activism** – we are busy with meet[ings] and activities, but this masks an e[mpty] spiritual life;
• **formalism** – we are concerned [with] structures and traditions witho[ut] passionate love for Jesus;
• **legalism or pharisaism** – we [are] concerned with comparisons, loo[king] good, church size and playing the [part] rather than faithfulness to God.

6. Jesus calls on the church to
• **'wake up and strengthen' (v 2)** [ie:] nurture spiritual life through the Wor[d of] God; and
• **'remember and repent' (v 3)** ie: [the] church must remember what it received and heard.

• **What has the church 'received a[nd] heard'?** The church received the gos[pel] message of Jesus our Lord and Savi[our] (see 1 Corinthians 15 v 1-8).

7. The church in Sardis is dead (v 1). [The] Holy Spirit is the Spirit of life. The H[oly] Spirit brings new life and renewal thro[ugh] the Word.

EXPLORE MORE: The Bible is written [by] human authors. But through their wo[rds] the Holy Spirit is speaking. The books [of] the Bible have a double authorship: [a] human author and the divine author. In t[he] Bible the Spirit is speaking to 'all of t[he] churches'.

There is a universal application of Scriptu[re] even if it is written in the first instance [to] particular people in particular histori[cal] contexts. In the Bible we hear what the Spirit 'is saying' continuously. It is not a dead letter, but a living voice.

- **What difference should these truths make?** See verse 3. We are to 'obey it'!

8. If the church does not repent, then Jesus will come like a thief in the night. This may be an allusion to the army of Cyrus, who centuries before had taken the city of Sardis unexpectedly by creeping up the cliffs. In the Gospels this is a reference to Jesus' second coming, but here it may mean His coming in history to remove the lampstand of Sardis, as He also warned He might do in Ephesus (2 v 5).

9. The risen Christ gives three promises to those who overcome:
- **'dressed in white' (v 4-5)** = an image of purity (see Revelation 7 v 13-14)
- **'walk with me' (v 4)** = see Genesis 3 v 8; 5 v 24; 6 v 9 = an image of friendship
- **'his name in the book of life' (v 5)** = see Revelation 20 v 11-15 = an image of security

10. There are a number of ways this question could be answered, but make sure they include:
- hearing and obeying the Word of God (v 3)
- relying on the work of the Holy Spirit (v 1)

Encourage people to identify practical steps they can take to do this.

11. Verse 1 shows us the danger of putting too much weight on reputation. Paul rated the commendation of God above the commendation of other people. But he also said church leaders should have a good reputation with outsiders (1 Timothy 3 v 7). We are to commend the gospel with our lives.

- **With whom should we have a good reputation?**
- **What are the dangers of a good reputation?**

OPTIONAL EXTRA

Ask local people what they think about your church and share their answers with the group. You could record a video 'vox pop' of people's responses.

Philadelphia: Revelation 3 v 7-13

THE PAIN OF EXCLUSION

BIG IDEA

Christians can feel that they are left out socially or are missing out materially, but Jesus promises much more in return.

SUMMARY

It seems the Christians in Philadelphia have been excluded from Jewish community life.

Jesus says the local synagogue belongs to Satan. The leaders of the synagogue may be ethnically Jewish, but they are no longer the true people of God (v 9). The church in Philadelphia is said to have 'little strength' (v 8), ie: it is small, unimportant and poor. But, despite its weakness, it has kept the Word of Jesus. Despite feeling they are left out or are missing out, they have not denied the name of Jesus (v 8).

Jesus has no word of condemnation and His only word of command is one they are already keeping – the command to keep going and to be patient (2 v 10). Instead, Jesus offers them a number of lovely encouragements.

1. **Jesus holds the key of David (v 7).** A key was a symbol of authority and responsibility. (It is still: young adults are given the keys of the house and successful people are given the keys of the city.) Jesus is given the authority of King David, ie: He is God's promised Saviour-King. The Jewish community in Philadelphia rejected the Christians and their Christ. But God has declared Jesus to be David's promised successor.

2. **Jesus opens a door to believers (v 7-8).** The Jewish community in Philadelphia had shut the door on the Christians (perhaps forbidding them from coming to the synagogue). But Jesus opens the door to His kingdom (see 4 v 1) and no one can shut it.

3. **Jesus will vindicate His people (v 9).** The Christians in Philadelphia must have wondered whether they were on the right side. The Roman Empire looked so strong and they had 'little strength'. The Jewish community had excluded them as heretics. But Jesus promises publicly to vindicate them. Isaiah promised a day when the Gentiles would bow before the Jews (Isaiah 60 v 14). But the Christians (both ethnic Jews and Gentiles) are the true Jews – the people of God.

4. **Jesus will keep his people (v 10).** 'The hour of trial' may be a coming crisis or it may be the events immediately before Christ's return. Either way, Jesus promises to keep His people (John 17 v 15).

5. **Jesus will include His people (v 12).** The Christians were excluded from the synagogue and cut off from the Jewish community. But Jesus will make them part of a new temple in a new Jerusalem. They will be pillars and no one can budge a pillar! They will never have to leave as they had to do from the synagogue.

Today Christians can often feel that they are left out (of, for example, friendship peer groups, office banter) or missing (on possessions, sex, marriage, success promotion). But Jesus promises much more in return.

GUIDANCE ON QUESTIONS

1-2. These examples can involve people in the group or stories they have heard about Christians elsewhere. Christians can often feel that they are left out (of, for example friendships, peer groups, office banter) or missing out (on possessions, sex, marriage success, promotion).

Pastoral note: listen carefully to what people say in this discussion – it may indicate particular struggles and temptations they are facing at the moment. Is there anything you will want to follow up on privately?

OPTIONAL EXTRA: Play a simple game or have a quiz. Tell people there will be prizes. But at the end give the prizes to the losers. We can often think of life as a game and worrying about losing out. Sometimes our Christian faith can feel like a handicap holding us back in the game of life. But the message of Jesus in Revelation 3 v 7–13 gives a very different perspective when we feel we are missing out. Use this as an introduction to questions 1 and 2.

3. The leaders of the synagogue may have

ethnically Jewish, but they are no longer the true people of God (v 9).

4. The church is said to have 'little strength' (v 8) – it was small, unimportant and poor. But, despite its weakness, it had kept the Word of Jesus. Despite feeling they were left out or missing out, they had not denied the name of Jesus (v 8).

5. This is an opportunity for people to make connections between the promises of Jesus and the feeling of exclusion the Christians felt. The following questions expand on these connections.

6. A key was a symbol of authority and responsibility. (It is still: young adults are given the keys of the house and successful people are given the keys of the city.) Jesus is given the authority of King David, ie: He is God's promised Saviour-King. The Jews in Philadelphia rejected the Christians and their Christ. But God has declared Jesus to be David's promised successor.

7. The Jewish community in Philadelphia had the shut the door on the Christians (perhaps literally forbidding them from coming to the synagogue). But Jesus opens the door to His kingdom (see 4 v 1) and no-one can shut it.

8. The Christians in Philadelphia must have wondered whether they were on the right side. The Roman Empire looked so strong and they had 'little strength'. The Jewish community excluded them as heretics. But Jesus promises publicly to vindicate them. Isaiah promised a day when the Gentiles would bow before the Jews (Isaiah 60 v 14). But the Christians (both Jews and Gentiles) are the true Jews – the people of God.

EXPLORE MORE. See verses 7, 15, 16-17. The beasts attack God's people and martyr those who refuse to worship them. They are also forbidden to buy and sell. As a result they miss out on the prosperity of the empire. In 2 v 9 Christians are excluded from the synagogue. In 13 v 17 they are excluded from the marketplace and miss out on prosperity.
• See especially verse 10. We are called to patient endurance and faithfulness. See also 14 v 12.

9. See verse 10. Jesus promises to keep those who obey his command to endure (John 17 v 15).

• **What is 'the hour of trial'?** 'The hour of trial' may be a coming crisis like a famine or persecution, or it may be the events immediately before Christ's return.

10. The Jewish Christians have had their status taken away. Now they are not only promised a crown, but a crown that no one will take away. The Christians were excluded from the synagogue and cut off from the Jewish community. But Jesus will make them part of a new temple in a new Jerusalem. They will be pillars and no one can budge a pillar! They will never have to leave as they had to do from the synagogue. 'Hold on, it won't be long,' people sometimes say. It is easy to hold on when we know it is only for a limited period. So Jesus in verse 11 says: 'I am coming soon. Hold on …'

EXPLORE MOVE: Christians no longer live for evil desires, but for God's will (v 1-2). So they no longer participate in the sinful behaviour of other people (v 3). As a result, old friends think Christians are strange and abuse them (v 4). Believers are to remember the example of Jesus (v 1) and remember that God will vindicate them (v 5).

☙ **Does your experience match what Peter describes?**

11. Try to summarise what the group has learned from the passage as a whole.

☙ **What should we remember in th times? What comfort does Je give?**

12. Often stating the negative help: clarify the positive. Not enduring m include giving up on Jesus, giving up church, keeping quiet about Jesus at v or giving in to temptation.

Laodicea: Revelation 3 v 14-22
THE DANGER OF SELF RELIANCE

BIG IDEA
We must never think we can live and grow as Christians without the constant help of Jesus.

SUMMARY
The city of Laodicea was famous for three things. First, it was *a banking centre*. And with that great wealth came a spirit of independence. The city was devastated by an earthquake in 61 AD, but refused imperial help. Second, it was *a medical centre* famous for its eye ointment. Third, it was *a clothing centre* famous for tunics made from local, glossy black wool.

Christianity is all about Christ. Jesus is 'the Amen, the faithful and true witness, the ruler of God's creation' (v 14). 'Amen' = truth. Jesus is the truth; God's 'yes' to God's promises. He is the maker of all things and the ruler of all things. The tragedy in Laodicea was that the church lived as though Jesus did not matter.

As a result, the church was effectively useless. Verses 15-16 refer to hot springs in

nearby Hierapolis that were channelled Laodicea. By the time the water reached city, it was lime-laden and tepid. It was hot enough to heal, nor cold enough refresh. We do not need to press the ana to decide what hot and cold might repres The point is the church was useless distasteful. Jesus is saying in effect: 'I am when I think about your church'.

The problem was the church was tryin live without Jesus (v 17). There had doubt been a time when the church seen its need of Jesus and come to Hir faith. But now the self-reliance of the had affected their attitude. They become comfortable, complacent and s satisfied. They had become so independ that Jesus was no longer at the cen Instead He was on the outside, knocl for re-admission. (Verse 20 has often b used to great effect in evangelism, bu was originally addressed to self-suffic Christians.)

This self-reliance is a form of self-decep (v 17). Laodicea was famous for its wea medicine and clothing. But spiritually speaking, the church in Laodicea was poor, blind and naked (v 17). The Christians in Smyrna were economically poor, but spiritually rich (2 v 9). In Laodicea they were economically rich, but spiritually poor.

Christ is about to spit the church out of his mouth (v 16). But He still loves them. His disciplining words and His disciplining absence are signs of His loving concern (v 19). He offers them gold for their spiritual poverty; clothes for their spiritual nakedness; and salve for their spiritual blindness. They do not need their banks, their clothing industry or their medical school. *They need Christ Himself.* Jesus offers them more than spiritual resources: He offers them Himself (v 20). He offers to eat with them – a powerful symbol of fellowship and friendship. Jim Elliott, the missionary martyr, famously said: 'He is no fool who gives what he cannot keep to gain what he cannot lose'.

GUIDANCE ON QUESTIONS

2. Jesus is 'the Amen, the faithful and true witness, the ruler of God's creation'. 'Amen' = truth. It is the word Jesus uses when He says: 'Truly, truly, I say to you' (often translated as: 'I tell you the truth'). Jesus is the truth, He is God's 'yes' to God's promises. In 2 v 13 Antipas is called a 'faithful witness' because he remained true to Jesus' name (see also chapter 11). But Jesus is the archetypal faithful witness: remaining faithful to death on the cross (1 v 5). And Jesus is the ruler of God's creation (1 v 5).

3. Jesus is the truth we should trust, the example we should follow and the ruler we should obey. He is also the one we need: the truth that sets us free, the witness whose death brings forgiveness and the ruler who keeps us.

4. We do not need to press the analogy to decide what hot and cold might represent. The point is the church was useless and distasteful. Jesus is saying in effect: 'I am sick when I think about your church.'

5. The church was 'wretched, pitiful, poor, blind and naked'. But perhaps the real problem was that it *thought* it was rich. It thought it had everything. It was self-satisfied, self-reliant and self-deceived. It said 'I am rich' when in fact it was spiritually poor.

EXPLORE MORE: It is good for Christians to feel their weakness when that leads to dependence on Christ. Christians should feel their own weakness, but have confidence in Christ's enabling power. We should not feel confident in ourselves (as if we do not need Christ), nor should we be debilitated by our weakness (as if Christ is not there to help). The problem in Laodicea was they did not think they needed Christ.

6. This self-reliance is a form of self-deception (v 17). Laodicea was a wealthy banking centre, but the church was wretched, pitiful and poor. Laodicea was a centre for eye care, but the church was blind. Laodicea was famous for its clothing, but the church was naked. The Christians in Smyrna were economically poor, but spiritually rich (2 v 9). In Laodicea they were economically rich, but spiritually poor.

7. The self-reliance of the city had affected the attitude of the church. It had become comfortable, complacent and self-satisfied. They had become so independent that Jesus was no longer at the centre.

• Look back at question 3. How was the influence of the world affecting the church's relationship to Jesus?

8. There are many ways in which this question could be answered. But you could focus on the similarities with the situation in Laodicea. Influenced by advertising, Christians often look to wealth and possessions for meaning and identity. Our health care is so advanced and comprehensive that we do not feel our need of God. Influenced by a focus on fashion, Christians often share our culture's obsessions with, and fears about, image and appearance.

OPTIONAL EXTRA: In connection with question 8, hand round some magazines – preferably magazines aimed at the kind of people in your group. Invite people to flick through the articles and adverts. As they read, ask them to shout out different things that our culture believes and values.

9. Jesus is on the outside, knocking for re-admission. It suggests He is no longer at the centre of church life. This self-reliant church does not think it needs Him.

• **Who is this verse addressed to?** Verse 20 has often been used to great effect in evangelism, but it was originally addressed to self-sufficient Christians.
• **Think of the Christians in Laodicea as a house. Where is Jesus? Is He on the inside or outside?**

10. Jesus is knocking for re-admission. He is offering to eat with people – a sign of fellowship and friendship. It shows us that, despite the poverty of this self-reliant church, Jesus still loves them. He is gracious. There is still hope for the church.

• **Where else in the message to t** church of Laodicea do we s **evidence for this?** See verse 19. T rebuke of Jesus is a sign of the love Jesus. He wants the Christians to repe and come back to Him.

11. Jesus offers Himself. He is gold for th spiritual poverty; clothing for their spirit nakedness; and healing for their spiritu blindness. What they really need is r their banks, clothing industry or medi school, but Christ Himself. They need learn again to rely on Christ. See also vers 20-21. Jesus offers to share a meal with – a picture of fellowship and friendsh And Jesus offers to share His throne with – a picture of honour and authority.

• **How does the imagery of verse reflect the glories of Laodicea?** Jes offers money to bankers, clothes fashion producers and eye salve doctors. His offer highlights the limits human self-reliance.

12. The 'products' that Jesus sells are fre We buy 'without money and without cos

• **Who does pay and what was th price?** Jesus paid the price of ou salvation and the price was His ow blood. See 1 Peter 1 v 18-19.

For further information about other Good Book Guides in this series, please contact The Good Book Company:
w: www.thegoodbook.co.uk   e: admin@thegoodbook.co.uk   t: 0845 225 0880

64 A message from Jesus to the church today | **LEADER'S GUIDE**